Published by UK Book Publishing
www.ukbookpublishing.com

ISBN: 978-1-915338-11-2

This book has been produced to support the teaching, learning and assessment processes of UK Breakin' members, reflecting the UK's experiences of Breakin'.

We advise all members to take part in additional health and safety training before attempting the actions in this book. There are Breakin' training sessions and classes taking place across the UK, and we advise all new learners to go to www.ukbreakin.org to find a teacher or training spot to learn the actions safely.

We will be working with teachers and judges to discuss and develop this book for future editions. We have worked in training spots in Wales, Scotland and England and welcome comments and feedback to improve for future editions.

We would like to collaborate with other breakers and other nations on Edition 2. If you'd like to get involved please email info@ukbreakin.org

#ByBreakersForBreakers #PlayingOurPart

BREAKIN UK⦁
HUBS

Find Your Local Hub >

Class hubs

- **Classes are led by UK Breakin' members. The members have DBS checks through UK Breakin', and take part in safeguarding training with UK Coaching. Our members are also developing accredited training together at Sunday sessions.**

Training hubs

- **Training hubs are UK Breakin' members-led. They tend to be adult sessions and don't necessarily have a safeguarding officer in place.**
- **Training sessions won't have one-to-one leaders, but there will be community support and the opportunity to train improvisation and new combinations.**

Keep up-to-date with UK Breakin' hubs at https://www.ukbreakin.org/hubs

2

Photographer

Pete Tweedie

www.petetweedie.com **@petetweedie**

Hi, I'm Pete and I've been shooting dance, among other things, for as long as I can remember.

I got my degree in photography because I find people amazing and fascinating and I want to capture that! How we interact with each other, how our values and beliefs shape us and how we live our lives.

The possibilities are infinite, seeing as we are all unique and I want to explore this through photography, to show you how I see the world and the people in it.

I always strive to create images that have a powerful impact, that showcase the personality and flavour of each dancer, that capture the essence and story behind each movement.

Showing people 'in the zone' of their passion is my passion, and I see each image as a chance to collaborate with the dancer so that we can bring you a story worth knowing.

3

Foreword

"For me looking back, the main thing that grabbed me about breakin' when I first saw it was it's lack of rules!

I mean it wasn't like other dances or sports where you had someone with a clip board telling you what to do.

It was street, it was dancing, it was styling and spinning with the freedom to express yourself with no rules or limits.

That was what made me fall in love with it!

It's different now. Everything changes, Everything evolves.."

Tony the Pencil, Second to None

Contents

Introduction to Breakin'

Breakin' is a part of Hip Hop Culture. A culture that encourages anti-segregation, inclusion, and expression.

"The South Bronx [in New York] had lost 600,000 manufacturing jobs, 40% of the sector disappeared. By the mid-seventies, average per capita income dropped to $2,430. The official youth employment rate hit 60%. Hip Hop Culture would arise from conditions of no work."

Chang J, 2007, Can't Stop won't Stop, Edition 2, Ebury Press, UK

Breakin' has been an artistic, sporting, and community activity in the UK since the 1980's.

We know that individuals started Breakin' in Manchester and in Newport in 1981. But Breakin' became a mass engagement activity in 1983, with 1000's of breakers seeing 'Flash Dance' and other movies such as 'Breakin'' and 'Beat Street', which encouraged people to get down. Breakin' was also featured in the opening ceremony of the LA Olympics in 1984 and on shows such as Top of the Pops.

Breakers travelled to the best spots to train their moves. Spots like Covent Garden in London, Madison Joes in Bournemouth, Brunel Rooms in Swindon, 'The Beer Gardens' in Cheltenham, Barry Island bumper car ride in Wales. Places that had the perfect floor for spinning.

The jazz dancers were rocking and locking before 1981 and many of these dancers developed Breakin' crews.

The history of Breakin' in the UK hasn't been documented and we are keen to work towards researching and recording the stories so that the efforts of the people who developed Breakin' in the UK are not lost.

Introduction to UK Breakin'

UK Breakin' is developing Breakin' as a membership organisation: building and connecting talent for sporting, artistic, and community opportunities.

We're doing this by highlighting, understanding, and developing pathways through participation for passionate people, and supporting the scene through training, accreditation, and recognition.

We're building an organisation for our culture to maintain integrity, essence, and respect by giving opportunities to those who need them. And developing a unified voice for the scene.

This Glossary of Terms has been developed by members meeting weekly, through social media interaction, and by connecting with international breakers for advice.

UK Breakin' members discussed how it is recognised in the scene, and that there are multiple names for many of the dance steps. Members have voted on which name should be the lead name for our teaching purposes and we've mentioned some of the names we know that have also been used.

A glossary is an alphabetical list of terms relevant to a certain field of study or action. So this glossary is a list of relevant words for UK breakers to develop teaching and learning, and to share our practice with each other and future audiences, participants, and partners.

While this is a collection of all terms, we need to take the time to learn in stages, so please use this as a guide to extending your knowledge at your own rate. UK Breakin' recommends learning these actions with an experienced breaker, and experienced breakers and teachers can be found on the website at www.ukbreakin.org/hubs

Hip Hop Terminology

Battles -

An event which hosts competitions.

Biting -

When someone copies a breaker's move/s, or a hip hop artist's art.

Call Outs -

When someone asks another to compete against them.

Cypher -

The circle formed to dance in.

Dope -

Something is very good.

East Coast -

The styles of Hip Hop created on the East coast of America.

Elements -

The art forms within Breakin' or within Hip Hop.

Flava -

Someone who has an interesting style.

Fly -

Someone who is dressed well.

Fresh -

Something new or exciting.

Get Down -

Someone who is dancing.

Hit the Beat -

When someone is in time with the music.

Jam -

An event where Hip Hop activity is taking place and people can participate.

Jamming -

People participating in a Hip Hop activity.

Levels -

How complex a move or situation is.

OG -

Describing the older generation.

Rounds -

Multiple turns in a jam, battle, or training session.

Sets -

Repeated combinations of actions or music combinations. Not all judges encourage sets in battles as they would like to see improvisation.

Sick -

Something is great.

Smoked -

When someone has won/beaten someone else in a competition.

Wack -

When something is bad.

West Coast -

Hip Hop Art created on the West coast of America.

Young Guns -

The youth (younger) generation.

General Breakin' Terminology

Bailing -
Falling or crashing out of a move.

Base -
The position for footwork, where both knees are bent and heels are off the floor.

Bonnie and Clyde -
A battle between a BBoy and a BGirl against another BBoy and BGirl.

Burns -
Someone making a gesture or a comment about another in a non-favorable way.

Chains -
A combination of up to five moves, not long in length so it isn't a set.

Commando -
When crew members transition in routines to continue the set, for example, by entrance and exit of the same move, working as a tag team.

Combos -
Describing moves linked together.

Concrete Battle -
A competition which takes place on concrete.

Crew -
A Breakin' crew is a collective of people, who train, battle, and support each other (a family).

Entrances -
A signature move or effective action to start a round, to make an impression as you enter the space.

Go for yours -

A phrase used to encourage breakers to win.

Footwork Battles -

A competition that is focused on footwork movements (with rules such as you cannot sit on your gluteus maximus).

Hip Hop Bounce -

Grooving and feeling the music in the body. The timing is guided by the beats in the music.

Hype -

The way to get the audience excited, but also to describe a dance style also known as 'New Jack Swing'.

Name -

BBoys and BGirls choose their own names that reflect their style and personality. Crews often choose names for individuals, or OG's give you a name.

Rock -

Grooving to the music. Standing feet slightly apart, knees relaxed and hips rock forward and back, chest rocks side to side. The timing is guided by the beats in the music.

Rocking / Up rock / Battle Rock -

A separate dance style often used during Toprock, created before Breakin' and which inspired original breakers.

Set -

A trained and rehearsed combination of moves that are performed at a battle.

Spiderman -

A position often used in footwork, a traditional position in footwork action.

Stab -

The position of the elbow into the body for freezes.

Stacking -

Linking freezes.

Tie Breaker -

When there is a split decision between the (judges?), this is a final round to decide the winner.

Throw Down -

A freestyle round.

Toprock -

A Toprock battle that involves only Breakin' Top actions.

7 to Smoke -

A competition where eight breakers battle, and the winner is the first person to beat all other seven people.

2v2 -

Two breakers take on two other breakers.

1v1 -

One breaker takes on another breaker.

Breakin' Style

Fashion is an important element of Breakin'. It allows breakers to achieve the best moves, with spin caps, beanies, bucket hats, spin jackets, and trainers all designed to achieve that aim.

Breakers have created their own fashion brands with people designing t-shirts, trainers and hats. Many designs are inspired by Graffiti art.

Designers in the UK include British Knights, Fat Laces, and Reebok. And spin caps designed by Second to None, Soapbox, Sterex, Street Scientists, and Swift Rock Classic Breakin'. Events have designed their own merchandise, and events such as Break Mission have multiple designs inspired by the themes of Hip Hop Culture.

Hip Hop popularised sportswear, bringing it into general casual wear. Breakin' uses fashion poses as part of the dance, for example, poses that highlight the brands breakers wear.

In the UK we have breakers such as Soopa J, who had sponsorship from sporting brands, promoting the newest tracksuits and trainers, and inspiring the next generation to buy the latest sports fashion.

Breakin' Styles

Breakin' styles are influenced by fashion, music and current trends, such as movies and cartoon characters. The biggest element of the style is the dancer's own personality, something they can show through expression, gestures, and actions. Bruce Lee and martial arts movies had a big influence on Breakin' and the development of the dance.

Examples of past and current styles are:

Abstract Styles -
A focus on flexibility, threads, and blow-ups.

Batman -
Inspired by the comic book character and the Batman cartoons.

Bugging out -
Reaching breaking point, where you release all the things that bug you and freestyle in a free creative way.

Caveman -
Moves include stomping on the floor, inspired by creative ideas of how cavemen move. There was a breaker in the LA Breakers called Caveman.

Character -
Breakers choose a character to imitate, such as a superhero or cartoon character.

Circus Styles -
Including more acrobatics in sets.

Clowning -
Not to be mistaken for the circus art of clowning or the original Krumpers, who also have a style called Clowning. Both use these styles to gesture and make fun of their opponents.

Crazy Commando -
Add additional 'crazy actions' taken from commando training, push-ups on knuckles, 6 steps on the back of the wrists, etc.

Drunken -
Inspired by Drunken Martial Art practice: "The more you drink the better you get".

European Style -
Early European style was all about the powermoves, little footwork and shorter sets built around power and freezes.
Flexible style -
Using actions that demonstrate the dancer's flexibility, splits, hollow backs, inverts, etc. The dancer also looks to create a unique position, demonstrating their flexibility. Inspired by Yoga.
Outlaw styles -
Made famous by Alien Ness. Additional step in Toprock moves. Potentially influenced by motorbike gangs.
Kung Fu -
The Kung Fu and other martial arts movies of the 1970s were popular viewing for breakers and inspired their styles.
Octopus -
Fluid actions, using movements inspired by how octopuses move.
Pistol Pete -
Pistol Pete was a famous basketball player. He used to spin to the floor, shooting pistols, and would stand back up and blow the smoke away. Breakers took his celebrations and added it to their Breakin'.
RAW -
An unpolished look, where actions are not performed with a clean technique.
Toronto Style -
Created by Canadian BBoys such as Bag of Trix and Supernaturals. The moves were made more complex, which created illusions in footwork and freezes.
West Coast -
A style created on the west coast of America.

Dance Terminology

Actions -
The movements the body makes.

Centreline –
The middle point of the body from head to feet.

Directions –
The way the body is facing, backing or travelling to.

Dynamics -
How the body moves, e.g. sharp, smooth, sudden.

Freestyle -
Dancing, responding to the music, not using previously performed sets.

Levels –
The level the action is performed compared to the ground.

Musicality –
The way the breaker reacts to the music, reacting to the beats, melody, and lyrics.

Routine -
A combination of choreographed moves linked together to show a range of action, space and dynamics.

Space -
The way the dancer uses the space through pathways, directions, levels, and formations.

Story Telling -
A structure type, where the dancer tells a narrative when performing.

Structure -
The order used to deliver a round.

Musicality

Beats –

The music to be played. Beats are divided into bars which create the time signature.

Breakbeats -

The music initially inspired by DJ Kool Herc, who linked instrumentals together to create lyric-free instrumentals to dance to. Breakbeats are created specifically for breakers to dance to.

Counting –

In a 4/4 rhythm dancers tend to count, "1,2,3,4,5,6,7,8" counting each crotchet.

Double time counting "1, and 2, and 3, and 4, and 5, and 6, and 7, and 8, and" counting each quaver.

Triple time counting "1, and a 2, and a 3, and a 4, and a 5, and a 6, and a 7, and a 8, and a" counting each semi-quaver.

These counts can also be acknowledged by teachers and choreographers by noises to highlight the beats they want actions to hit, varying speeds and adding different dynamics.

Dance on Beat -

Hitting the rhythm (focusing on the snares), but also other highlights within the music.

Flava -

Music that has an inspiring style.

Killing the Beat -

A dancer demonstrating a high level of interpreting the music.

Time Signature –

Not all music is in 4/4 rhythm so the counting by dancers won't always count up to 8, for example 3/4 music would be counted 1,2,3. 6/8 time signature would be counted 1,2,3,4,5,6.

Style –

The name *Breakin'* was inspired by the dancers moving to the instrumental BREAKS in the music.

Warm Up Exercises

Actions to prevent injury and prepare the body for the post-training rest.

Breathing -

Breathing exercises can regulate the right amount of oxygen to prepare and perform Breakin' actions.

Example exercises: Lying down and taking a deep breath, holding for a moment, and then releasing slowly.

Cardiovascular -

Making blood circulate faster around the body to increase the amount of oxygen getting to the muscles.

Example exercises: From walking at increased speed to running around the room.

Isolations -

Preparing joints for exercise and movement, by enabling synovial fluid.

Example exercises: Gently rotating wrists clockwise and anti-clockwise.

Strengthening -

Preparing muscles and joints for the impact they will experience when Breakin'.

Example exercises: Squats.

Stretching -

Preparing muscles for exercise and reducing the build-up of lactic acid. Including Dynamic and Static stretches.

Example exercises: Sitting up and placing arms behind, lifting legs up to the nose, and then dropping to the ground away from each other.

Activity preparations

Preparing for Breakin' includes many lifestyle choices.

Activity preparations includes healthy lifestyle choices such as drinking water to stay hydrated, getting the right amount of sleep / rest.

Conditioning joints and muscles to prepare them for actions, to prevent injury, and recover from repetitive actions.

It is advised to do conditioning on both sides of the body so that you can prevent the overdevelopment of one side.

Ankle strengthening -

Ankle raises, lowering, and raising the ankles first one at a time and then both together.

Core strengthening -

Sit-ups, press-ups, plank to work core strength.

Dynamic Stretches -

Stretches that move in and out of the stretch with fluid dynamics, they do not hold the stretching position.

Mental Preparation -

Visualising the moves you wish to perform or combine, to mentally prepare for the action.

Research -

Knowledge is an important part of Hip Hop Culture.

Sleep -

Achieve deep sleep by making sure there is fresh air in the room, through plants or opening windows. Take naps when the body is tired as training when tired can increase injury.

Static Stretches -

Stretches held in certain positions, to stretch specific muscles.

Wrist strengthening -

Rotating, stretching, and weight-baring as part of warm-ups.

Prerequisistes exercises

Exercises that are practiced before attempting the full actions.

It is advised to do these exercises to train the muscles needed to perform the actions, to reduce the risk of injury.

Duck Walks -

Practicing base, walking forwards and backwards, preparing knees for footwork.

Flare Prep -

There are many preparation activities for flare, based on rotating hips, kicking legs, and catching the body behind the back when sitting.

Handstand -

In handstand, practice holding a two-handed handstand for two minutes. When confident with two hands, practice one-handed on both hands.

Headspin prep -

In a headstand (making a triangle with the head and both hands), rotate the legs side-to-side a foot in contact on the floor and hips above shoulders.

Power prep -

Taking the weight between hands and feet to prepare for falling and catching moves in the hands and feet in power moves.

Tipping-

In base, practice touching the floor, front, back, and side.

Safety Basics

Space -

Ensure the floor is clear.

Find places and spaces which have safeguarding in place, check out the red hubs on the website www.ukbreakin.org/hubs

Clothes -

Where tops to cover the shoulders.

For spinning find material that slides.

Practicing headspins or taking weight on the head use beanie hats.

There is specialist Breakin' clothing brands where you can buy specific trainers, caps, spin tops, etc. These have often been designed by breakers and can help perform the actions and reduce the risk of injury,

Take your time -

Taking time to build strength and flexibility, through regular training, will reduce the risk of injury. Practice other healthy lifestyle measures to support regular training.

The Level Key

This glossary has been written in alphabetical order and broken into types of actions.

We have associated a colour with each move. The colour relates to the suggested difficulty level of the action. Each body is different. Some bodies will find it possible to achieve some Level Two actions at Level One. The Level has been suggested based on the level of strength, flexibility and coordination needed to achieve the move.

Level One

Level Two

Level Three

Level Four

Level Five

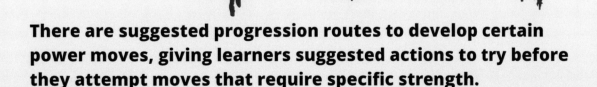

There are suggested progression routes to develop certain power moves, giving learners suggested actions to try before they attempt moves that require specific strength.

Level Three upwards we suggest you learn with a UK Breakin' teacher.

There is also space to write your own combinations and training strategies.

Toprock

The standing actions in Breakin', establishing the groove using bounces and rocks within the steps, linked to the music being played.

Risks -

General risks with Toprock are: turning over on the ankle, twisting knees, jarring the lower back. We advise you to warm up before and regularly use ankle-conditioning exercises.

Ali Shuffle

Actions –

Five kicks forward, kick one leg, then the other on the beat and then three quick-kicks forward, double time. A version of the Hustle kick.

Timing –

1, 2, 3 and 4.

History -

Muhammad Ali, arguably the best heavyweight boxer of the 20th century, used a similar action to this as he fought. This move is a tribute, inspired by him. A doubled up version of the Hustle kick.

Back Step

Action -

Flick one leg forward, step on that leg feet, tap back on the other leg, flick that other leg forward to repeat on the other side.

Timing –

1 and 2

CC Step

Action –

Dropping onto the one foot, bending the other leg and twisting with the knee inverting. The bent leg leaves the lifted inverted position and flicks forward, straight. Then you drop onto the now straightened leg to repeat on the other leg.

Timing –

1 and 2.

Many steps done in Toprock have been modified to do at other levels and vice versa. There will be moves such as CC that you will see in Back Rock, Footwork, etc.

Charlie Rock

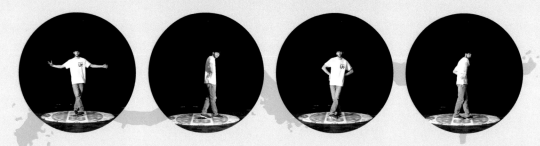

Action–

One leg taps forward, swing that leg behind, switching weight to use the leg. Other leg taps behind and then swing that leg forward, e.g. right tap forward, right step back, left tap back, left step forward. Keep weight on the balls of the foot and the foot positions. The ankle swivel on the beat and count.

Timing –

1 and 2 and 3 and 4 and.

Variations -

Singles and Doubles.

History -

Inspired by the Charleston.

Cross Over Step

Action –

One leg flicks forward, land on that leg while flicking the other leg forward. Keep that leg lifted and cross over and land onto it, land back on the other leg keeping the leg that crossed over lifted. Swap onto the other side. Hips will twist side-to-side but keep head and chest forwards.

Timing –

1, 2, 3, 4.

Variation –

Kick Cross Step (Around the World, Circular Step).
Action – As you lift the leg you cross over, you circle the leg from the knee before kicking it forward.

History -

(Shuffles / Indian Step/ Indian Crossover / Brooklyn Shuffle/ Kick Cross Step)
BBoy POW WOW's "Ain't no Indian step! It's my step!".
Pow Wow states the Latinos called it a CROSS OVER step.

Cross Step

Action –

Is based on the two-step, but one leg crosses over the other. Once the leg crosses and then both legs jump back together, then the other leg crosses over. Arms swing open as the leg crosses.

Timing –

1, 2.

History –

Also known as Indian step, Aha, Plain Tops, and Ken Swift calls this step Two on Top.

Cross Back Step

Action –

Is based on the two step, but one leg crosses behind the other. Once the leg crosses and then both legs jump back together, then the other leg crosses over. Arms swing open as the leg crosses.

Timing –

1, 2.

Crouched Toprock

This is when you use Toprock steps at a lower level, with bent knees.
Toprock can be done at different levels. The music will have different influences, for example Raw Power and Too Fitness Top Rock.

Heel and Toe

Action –

Weight on the heel of the front foot and toe of the back foot and both rotate outwards, e.g. if the right foot is in front the right foot toes twist to the right off the floor and the left heel twists to the left off the floor, hips twist to the right. Bring feet together and then step the other foot in front to repeat on the other side.

Timing –

1 and 2.

Hussle Step

Action –

Kick one leg, then the other, and the original leg, step onto that leg, side on the other and behind with the original to turn the body towards the direction you came from and repeat on the other side. Use the right arm when starting on the right and left arm when starting on the left.

Timing –

1, 2, 3 and 4.

History -

Also known as Time step and Latin Rock. Lockers and Rockers both used the step but used different names for the action.

March Step

Action –

Stepping one leg, then the other, while travelling forward or back. Knees are not lifted too high, allowing rotations in the hips to allow the knee of the lifted leg to rotate away from the centre line of the body.

Timing –

1, 2.

History –

Step often performed to Apache music, also known as the Apache, Skate or Breathers.

Original Toprock

Action –

See Cross Step, but allow the leg to kick back before you jump with your feet together.

History –

Also known as Original Indian Step, or Traditional Toprock.

Pas de Bourrée

Action –

Larger step to the side with one leg, then step the other leg in so both feet are together, step to the side with the original leg. Repeat to the other side.

Timing –

1 and 2.

Salsa Step

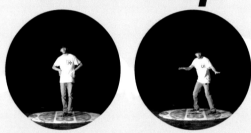

Action –

One leg flicks forward and steps in, the other foot taps out to the side transferring the weight partly before stepping weight fully back onto the supporting leg. Repeat on the other side.

Timing –

1 and 2 and.

Variation –

Side direction can be taken forwards, side backwards and diagonally. The kick can go to the back or there can be no kick at all.

History -

Puerto Rican influence in Breakin' from the early days in the Bronx.

Step Ups

Action –

Moving toward your opponent, moving back leg gradually towards the leg which is closest the opponent.

Variation –

Can end in a pose or a Getdown.

Tell the Time

Action –

Rocking step forwards, flick one foot forwards, place back into place to transfer the weight to step forwards with the other leg. 'Look at your watch' as you step forwards and as you step back point forwards at your opponent.

Timing –

1 and 2.

Toprock Wiggle

Action –

Cross Step, but instead of jumping back, step feet slightly together. Arms relaxed and knees and hips wiggled side-to-side then Cross Step the other side to repeat.

Timing–

1, and a 2.

Turning Toprock

Action –

Toprock steps when changing direction (often Cross Step changing feet), also known as four corners, as you look to four different corners as you make the turn.

Two Step

Action –

One leg taps out and steps feet together, the other taps leg out and steps feet together, repeated, the step doesn't cross the body. Weight is on the front of the feet.

Timing –

1, 2.

Variation –

Can be taken in any direction. Can be changed so the step happens and the foot taps the feet together, so that the foot is ready to step straight after. This allows the move to travel the weight side-to-side.

Rocking / Uprock

A separate dance style often used as part of Toprock

Breathers (Brooklyn Rock)

Action –

Kick one leg forward, hop twice on the supporting leg, jump into an ankle hook.

Timing –

1 and 2.

Variation –

Kick one leg forward, kick the other leg forward and jump into ankle hook.

Jerks

Action –

Hips pushed back arms forward, hips push forward arms on hips, drop to base.

Timing –

1 and 2.

Will Power

Action –

Step one leg forward and then switch both feet taking the original forwards leg to the back and bringing other leg forward in one action. Then hips rock forward back and drop down bending both knees.

Timing –

1, 2, 3 and 4.

Variations

All Toprock can be considered Level Five. To achieve Level Five your form would be perfect and you would be being creative with the actions trying different levels, and additions such as spins, threads or gestures for example.

Toprock is an element where you can practice different Breakin' styles or demonstrate your own personality. This can also be creative and add to the difficulty level.

Great international examples would be BBoy YNot, or in the UK, BGirl Leebee or BBoy RawB.

Gestures / Burns

Actions generally done with hands and arms.

Risks –

The general risks with using Burns are if they are regarded as inappropriate for the competition. In league competitions, you will be marked down for the use of inappropriate Burns based on the audience the competition will reach.

Bailing
You fell, crashed, failed.

Biting
Copying someone else.

Counting fingers.
How many times have you repeated that move / set.

Shove it

It's over.
Ive won!

Slashes.
Inspired by martial arts
sword play.

Ummmm!
Didn't get that right!

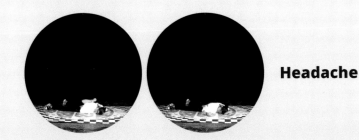

Headache

Breakin' is about showing yourself and self-expressing. On some days this is showing frustration, as breakin' allows you to learn to control your energy and emotions.

Go Downs / Drops
Actions generally used to go from standing to the floor.

Risks –

General risks with Go Downs relate to crashing and bumping joints and muscles on the floor, which can lead to bruising and long-term damage. To reduce the risk it is important to work on control to prevent things like your knees hitting the floor when they should be kept up, or breath control to fall with an exhale to allow for the movement to continue with less tension in the muscles.

Coin Drop

Action –

Place one hand on the floor in front of you making a V with the two feet placed on the ground. Thread the other arm through, make one rotation on your back.

Timing –

1, 2.

Variations –

1) Thread straight into the backspin without placing the arms.
2) Start on knees.

History –

Also known as Chinos named after Action / Chino.

Corkscrew

Action –

Step forward, twist on the balls of both feet half a turn, bend the back knee and bring the original front leg into a tucked position behind, continue to turn another half turn.

Timing –

1, 2.

Cross Step Go Down

Action –

Cross over like in Toprock and from the crossed position, leave feet crossed, twist hips to the front and drop onto both knees.

Timing –

1 and 2, 3.

Variation –

To protect the knees, use knee drop not to drop onto knees.

Fake Flare

Action –

Rock back on leg to prepare, place hand on the floor, kick leg drags through and leg releases in the air.

Timing –

1, 2.

Hook Drop

Action –

Step forward as in Two Step or Cross Step, bring front leg to back leg hooking in front as you dropdown.

Timing –

1, 2.

Front Half Sweep

Action –
Sweep leg into a hook as you bend the supporting knee and lower a hand to the ground.

Timing –
1.

Variation –
Back sweep as you lower.

Front Sweep Hook

Action –
Step onto one leg, to hop on that leg bringing the other knee up as you hop, step onto the leg you just bent the knee of, drop down and then sweep.

Timing –
1, 2, 3, 4.

Knee Drop

Action –

Tuck one foot behind the opposite knee and bend the supporting leg until both feet are touching the floor.

Timing –

1, 2.

Top tip:

When initially learning, practice with the hand out to be able to support the balance as you drop.

Knee Slide

Action –

Prepare so the weight is on one foot, place the hand down, slide the same arm as leg through, and make sure not to let the knee make contact with the floor as you slide the leg through.

Timing –

and 1.

Lazy Get Down

Action –

Step forward on one leg, tuck the other leg behind, place the same arm as leg tucking on the floor and lie down (head last).

Timing –

1, 2.

Over Under Go Down

Action –

Place arm down on the floor by the opposite leg, the leg closest to the arm goes over the top of the other leg on the floor. The leg from the floor goes on top in the figure four position. Hook that top leg underneath the supporting leg and drag hop in this position into a hook at base level.

Timing –

1 2 and 3 4.

History –

Also known as Scissor Sweep.

45

Rummenigy

Action –

Place hand on the floor. Same leg as the hand on the floor sweeps through on the knee, keep the weight on the outside of the calf and switch so both knees face the right, weight on the other hand at the back and bring the same knee (as weight on hand) more forwards than the original leg and weight on supporting hip.

Timing –

1 and 2.

Swing to Corkscrews

Action –

Cross Step forward, circle the leg into a back hook, and corkscrew down.

Timing –

1, 2, 3.

Variations –

Cross Step back and ankle hook in front to corkscrew down. The corkscrew can reverse to return back to standing.

Torpedo Dive

Action –

Step forwards on non-dominant leg, punch opposite arm forwards, at a 45 degree angle to create a circular movement onto shoulder blades, neck tucked in to protect neck and head, concave chest.

Timing –

1, 2, 3, 4.

Twist Drop

Action –

Feet apart, with both feet facing one direction, twist the hips and feet and drop onto the back leg while the front knee stays off the ground.

Timing –

1, 2.

Drop Freezes

Actions generally used to go from standing to a Freeze position.

Risks –

The general risks with Drop Freezes relate to crashing and bumping joints and muscles on the floor, which can lead to bruising and long-term damage. To reduce the risk it is important to work on control to prevent things like wrist injuries when landing in these positions from Toprock or Power moves.

Back Wide Kick-Out

Action –

From standing, drop to base, kick legs out into wide V behind.

Timing –

1 and 2, 3.

Back Wide Kick-Out
(with zip up)

Action –

From standing, drop to base, kick legs out into wide V behind, then zip legs together.

Timing –

1 and 2.

Back Wide Kick-Out
(with point)

Action –

From standing, drop to base, kick legs out into wide V behind, stretch one arm out through your legs with a point at your opponent.

Timing –

1 and 2.

Front High Kick-Out

Action –
From standing, drop to base, kick legs out into a smaller V.

Timing –
1 and 2.

Front Small Kick-Out

Action –
From standing, drop to base, kick legs out to one side creating a V with hand in contact with the floor and both feet.

Timing –
1 and 2.

Front Wide Kick-Out

Action –
From standing, drop to base, kick legs out into wide V.

Timing –
1 and 2.

James Brown

Action –

Kick one leg forward, diagonally and hop, place leg that kicked forwards diagonally back and slide front leg forwards to land in half splits.

Timing –

1 and 2.

History –

Breakin' like Break Beats took inspiration from James Brown, who was famous for a half split move he performed as he sang. This move is performed recognise James Brown's influence in Hip Hop.

Side Close Kick-Out

Action –

From standing, drop to base, kick legs out to one side creating a V with hand in contact with the floor and both feet, then zip both feet together.

Timing –

1 and 2, 3.

Side Wide Kick-Out

Action –

From standing, drop to base, kick legs out to one side creating a V with hand in contact with the floor and both feet.

Timing –

1 and 2.

W-Freeze

Action –

Drop both knees forward, push hips forward, place one hand behind.

Timing –

1.

Footwork

Actions generally done with the feet at base level. Hands are in a choice of two positions: 1) flat hands or fingers, and 2) thumbs in contact.

Risks –

The general risks with Footwork include long-term damage to knees from stopping in the base position. Ensuring strengthening exercises are part of the conditioning is essential. Other injuries might include bruises from hitting the floor and potential straining of wrists or ankles. Conditioning and technique exercises will be the best way to prevent these injuries. In finger and thumb position (Footwork hands) there is a greater risk of dislocating thumbs.

Around the Worlds

Action –

From base, stay in base, place one hand on the floor and travel towards that arm forwards, place the other arm on the floor and continue to spin.

Timing –

1 and 2 and.

Variations –

Continuous.

History –

Also known as Zulu s, continuous Zulus, or Tornados.

Back Baby Switches
(Cross actions)

Action –
Similar to Back Shuffles – resting in baby freeze, leg open, cross, open, switch to the other arm stay in baby freeze legs open, cross, open and switch to repeat.

Timing –
1 and 2 and 3 and 4 and.

Back CC's / Trac-2 Shuffles

Action –
Starting in Spiderman, land on one leg, relax other knee into leg baring weight flicking that foot to create a C shape. Then step onto the lifted leg, step onto the other leg to balance weight, step onto the next leg to be able to lift the other leg into the C shape, both knees relaxed throughout.

Timing –
1 and 2 and.

Back Shuffle

Action –

From Spiderman, legs switch in and out, crossing a different foot in front each time.

Timing –

1 and 2 and.

Big Sweep

Action –

Make a ¼ of the Flare Rotation, kick the one leg to the side, instead of lifting the second leg, sweep the leg through and land on your gluteus maximus.

Timing –

1, 2, 3.

Bicycle Pump's

Action –

Starting from Spiderman, knee bends into abdominals and switch to the other leg, and again.

Timing –

1 and 2.

Boyong Switches

Action –

From base, extend one leg forward, same arm and extended leg touches the floor. Hop the leg in base into a hook position, twisting the body to face the arm on the floor and traveling the body forwards. Hop back to the same leg being in base, and switch to repeat on the other side.

Timing –

1, 2, 3.

Bum Sweep

Action –

Starting on all fours, lift the one leg behind the other hooking the knee after crossing. Rotate on the leg that crossed using the shin, and rotate the body 360 degrees. Put the weight onto the knee of the other leg to allow the leg that was rotating on the shin to lift to the front right onto the foot.

Timing –

1, 2, 3.

Collapse

Action –

Often used during Footwork. Collapse onto stomach and tap the floor twice with a fist.

Timing –

1, and a.

Corkscrew Up

Action –
From Footwork, cross one foot over the other and rotate to standing.

Timing –
1, 2.

Curly Shuffle / Homer Simpson

Action –
Weight on one shoulder, run legs around the outside. Allow the body to circle on the spot.

Timing –
1, and 2, and 3, and 4, and.

History –
Inspired by cartoon character, Homer Simpson.

CC's

Action –

From base, extend one leg forwards and place the same arm as extended leg to the floor to the side and slightly back. Twist towards extended leg, while bringing both knees together. Send the non-extended leg foot to the ceiling creating a C shape, transfer that leg back to base and switch to repeat the other side.

Timing –

1 and 2, 3 and 4.

History –

Also known as Switches, taps and originally Russian taps. CC refers to Crazy Commandos the Crew and the step.

Variations –

Varying the level, low to high. Add additional rotations.

Crazy Commando Footwork

Actions –

A mixture of Footwork steps, but including additional actions such as Footwork on the forearms, on using knuckles instead of hands, adding push ups, extending actions to see how big you can reach in Footwork.

History –

It is related to a crew in New York called the Crazy Commando Crew, who made moves harder and invented moves such as the CC.

Direction Shuffles

Action –

From base, put one hand to the ground and kick legs forward one after the other, swap hands and repeat, and rotate as you repeat.

Timing –

1 and 2.

Forward Roll

Action –

Tuck head in, hands on the floor, roll onto both shoulder blades. Keep a tucked position and rotate until head in back upright.

Timing –

1, 2, 3, 4.

Four Corners exercise

Action –

In base, move the hands into different positions. One hand in between the feet, swap hands, move original hand behind the same heel as hand, other hand behind same heel as hand and repeat. Put weight onto hands each time and allow the hips to move and rotate as you swap hands.

Timing –

1 and 2 and.

Front Swing Shuffle

Action –

From base, half sweep / swing leg towards a hook position but stop before the hook, placing the weight onto supporting hand and swap to half sweep and swing the other leg.

Timing –

And 1, and 2.

Variations –

Front Swing Shuffle over Knees and Front Swing Shuffle under knees.

High Switches

Action -

From base, put one hand on the ground and kick legs forward as high as possible, one after the other, swap hands and repeat, and rotate as you repeat.

Timing –

1 and 2.

Hooks

Action –

Wrapping one leg around the other, either around the ankle or over the knee.

Timing –

1.

History –

This has also become a focused style, where people use hooks in all Footwork steps.

Kick Outs

Action –

From base, place one hand on the floor and kick both legs out and in together.

Timing –

and 1.

Variations –

The move can go in multiple directions.

Kip Up

Action –

Rock back onto the shoulders, hands placed behind the shoulders. Tuck knees into chest, push your legs at a 45 degree angle, allow the hips to push forwards, followed by the chest to come to standing.

Timing –

1, 2.

Kip Up – twist baby facing backward of where you started

Action –

Rock back onto the shoulders, hands placed behind the shoulders. Tuck knees into chest, push your legs at a 45 degree angle, allow the hips to push forwards, to base position. Twist the body to rotate to land in a Baby Freeze (see Baby Freeze).

Timing –

1, 2.

Kip Up –
throwing forward to press up

Action –

Rock back onto the shoulders, hands placed behind the shoulders. Tuck knees into chest, push your legs at a 45 degree angle, allow the hips to push forwards, to base position. Fall forwards to land into press up position.

Timing –

1, and 2.

Variations –

Don't land in base position in-between, tuck feet under and land in press up.

Knee Rock

Action –

12 step on your knees. Travelling in a circle around hands on the floor (when travelling anti-clockwise) step left, right, left knee, right knee and repeat.

Timing –

1, and a 2, and a 3, and a 4, and a 5, and a 6, and a.

History –

Also related to a style, Knee Rock Style, which took Footwork steps onto the knees.

No handed Run - Mario

Action –

From base, take to the air in a running stance or leg to each side, legs reaching to each hand.

Timing –

1, 2.

History –

Ken Swift Rock Steady Concept.

Pretzels

Action –

From being on two knees, sweep one leg backwards and around while your weight goes onto opposite hand. Transfer weight onto the same arm as leg as you lift the other knee to allow the sweeping leg to travel under to complete the circle. Tuck the circling leg behind the other leg, with both hands on the floor. Rotate the body in the direction of the hook to place the other knee onto the floor and to repeat the other side.

Timing –

1 and 2, 3 and 4.

History –

Also known as Knee Sweeps.

Variations –

66

Backward (where the sweep starts by travelling under the knee).

Reaching

Action –

During Footwork, pause during and extend one arm towards a point further away from the opposite foot and recover.

Timing –

1, 2.

Russian

Action –

From base, kick one leg and then the other forwards, with your hands off the floor.

Timing –

1 and.

History –

Inspired by Russian Dance. Also known as Dose Step, created by BBoy DOse in the 1980's. [Delete? reference to] Ken Swift

Side Rolls

Action –

Starting on hands and knees, collapse onto one shoulder. Use a diagonal line to roll onto the right shoulder, allow the knees to follow and finish in front of the body.

Timing –

1, 2.

Variations –

Instead of collapsing, thread the arm through in between the opposite hand and knee.

Side Straight Leg Shuffle

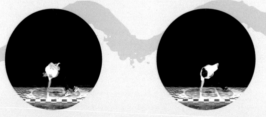

Action –

Jump both feet from base to the side of the body, one foot in front of the other, then switch. Keep the opposite hand to the direction of the feet on the floor.

Timing –

1 ,2, 3, 4.

Sweeps

Action –

Using one leg to sweep the other leg out of the way. By starting on all fours, take one leg under the knee of the other, lifting the same hand as the leg to make room, circle the leg fully to finish where it started.

Timing –

1, 2.

Variations –

Reverse Sweep, where the leg circles before it crosses under the supporting knee.
Sweeps with knee off the floor.

Sweep Pivots

Action –

Facing to a front diagonal, one leg extended forwards, sweep that leg around with weight on the same hand as sweeping. Hop on to the other leg to sweep the other leg, changing the weight onto the other hand. Allow the body to rotate at the same time.

Timing –

1, 2.

Thread - basic

Action –

Creating a hole and putting a limb through it. Make a hole by connecting a limb to another part of the body, or a limb to floor. Threads are a concept often used in Footwork, but also can also be used in freezes and in power.

Timing –

1, 2.

Threads are a concept and can be taken to Level Five depending on when and how they are used.

Toe Rock Shuffle

Action –

From Spiderman, place a toe onto the floor, hook the other leg under in front of the ankle just placed and twist the hooked leg and head towards each other and away.

Timing –

1,2,3.

Traditional Footwork Track
(Head Swipes)

Action –
Starting from a figure four Chair Freeze, rotate away from the stabbing arm, kicking the opposite leg from the stabbing arm in a circular motion to land in the same Chair Freeze or Baby Freeze, keeping your head in contact with the floor the whole time.

Timing –
1, 2, 3.

Variations –
1 leg

Two-Handed Switches

Action –
A CC but taking both hands to one side of the body as you CC.

Timing –
And 1, and.

W Circles

Action –

From base, push hips forward and lower one hand back as the hips going forwards. As you recover rotate and then push the hips to another direction, continue recover, and rotate action in a circle.

Timing –

1, and 2, and 3, and 4, and.

History –

Ken Swift Foundation – a cross between Knee Rock and W Freeze.

1 Step
(Helicopter, Coffee Grinder)

Action –

From base, one leg rotates from base position missing the hook and swinging around and under supporting leg and out to the side. Hands stay on the floor slightly at the front and lift to allow the leg to pass.

Timing –

1, 2.

Variations –

Helicopter (Reverse).
Helicopter (UFO).
Helicopter (Line).
Helicopter (Custom no hands, 1 hand, stop n goes, shin, change direction).

2 Step

Action –

From base, extend one leg forwards, swing into a hook, swap hands and direction, kick opposite leg forward, switch extended led and repeat from the hook.

Timing –

1, and 2, and.

History –

Created by Lil' Julio from Crazy Commandos, also known as Salsoul Float and Baby Swipes.

3 Step

Action –

From base, extend one leg forwards, switch legs and hook this extended leg. Place both hands on the floor and jump feet out to create a small Spiderman position, repeat facing the other side.

Timing –

1, 2, 3.

History –

Created by Batch from the Bronx Boys.

4 Step

Action –

From base, hop one leg back, then switch legs at the back. Hop forwards on the same leg then switch legs at the front.

Timing –

1.

History –

Created by JoJo from Rock Steady Crew and Crazy Commandos.

5 Step

Action –

From base, extend one leg forwards, switch legs and hook this leg. Place weight onto the hooking leg, stretch the other leg onto the back diagonal, step the hooking leg into Spiderman position.

Timing –

1, and 2, and.

6 Step

Action –

From base, hook one leg and place weight onto the hooking leg. Stretch the other leg onto the back diagonal, place hooking leg into Spiderman position. Stretch the other leg from the back diagonal and to the opposite front diagonal, tuck the hooking leg into the front leg, unhook the front leg and back to base.

Timing –

1, 2, 3, 4, 5, 6.

Variations –

Different directions.
Change levels as you take each step.

7 Step

Action –

From base, hook one leg and place weight onto that hooking leg. Stretch the other leg onto the back diagonal, stretch the hooking leg to Spiderman position. Stretch the other leg from the back diagonal to the opposite front diagonal, then step leg from back diagonal over the top of the straight leg currently in front diagonal. Kick the back leg to base, then the other leg to base.

Timing –

1, 2, 3, 4, 5, 6, and.

8 Step

Action –

From base, hook one leg and place weight onto that hooking leg. Stretch the other leg onto the back diagonal, tap the same leg that went back from the back diagonal straight forwards then step back to where it originally stepped back to. Stretch the hooking leg to the Spiderman position, then step the tapping leg back diagonally through to front diagonal. Tuck the back leg into the front leg by the knee, unhook the front leg back to base.

Timing –

1, 2, 3, 4, 5, 6, 7, 8.

9 Step

Action –

From base, hook one leg and place weight onto that hooking leg. Stretch the other leg onto the back diagonal, tap the same leg that went back from the back diagonal straight forwards then step back to where it originally stepped back to. Stretch the hooking leg to the Spiderman position, then step the tapping leg from back diagonally through to front diagonal. Then step leg from back diagonal over the top of the straight leg currently in front diagonal, kick the back leg to base, then the other leg to base.

Timing –

1, 2, 3, 4, 5, 6, 7, 8, and.

10 Step

Action –

From base, hook one leg and place weight onto that hooking leg. Stretch the other leg onto the back diagonal, tap the same leg that went back from the back diagonal straight forwards, then step back to where it originally stepped back to. Stretch the hooking leg to the Spiderman position. Crisscross the legs by switching them at the back and unswitch them. Then step the tapping leg from back diagonally through to front diagonal, then step leg from back diagonal over the top of the straight leg currently in front diagonal. Kick the back leg to base, then the other leg to base.

Timing –

1, 2, 3, 4, 5, 6, and 7, 8, and.

11 Step

Action –

From base, hook one leg and place weight onto that hooking leg. Stretch the other leg onto the back diagonal, tap the same leg that went back from the back diagonal straight forwards then step back to where it originally stepped back to. Stretch the hooking leg to the Spiderman position. Crisscross the legs by switching them at the back and unswitch them twice. Then step the tapping leg from back diagonally through to front diagonal, then step leg from back diagonal over the top of the straight leg currently in front diagonal. Kick the back leg to base, then the other leg to base.

Timing –

1, 2, 3, 4, 5, and 6, and 7, 8, 1 and 2.

12 Twelve Step

Action –

From Spiderman (push up position, knees relaxed, neutral
with both hands on the floor. Feet step – cross over, side,
cross back, side three times. Hands stay on the floor and feet
create a circle.

Timing –

1, and 2, and 3, and 4, and 5, and 6, and 7, and.

History –

Also known as Baby Love named after the Rock Steady
Manager and Running Shuffles.

Floor Rock

Actions are generally Footwork performed while the dancer is lying on their back / shoulders.

Back Rock

Action –

From lying on your back, twist to one side with the opposite arm going over the top of you to the floor, the palm of the hand flat to act as a support. Make a right angle shape with the shoulder and arm you are lying on. The leg you are lying on becomes the supporting foot as you twist your gluteus maximus to the air, lifting your knees off the ground and your nonsupporting foot to the sky (but keep your knees together). Roll back on your back, but lift hips off the floor by placing the leg which was in the air onto the ground. Switch legs to roll and repeat on the other side.

Timing –

1 and 2.

Variation –

'Over the Log' Back Rock steps that leaps over the leading leg.

Back Rock High

Action –

From lying on your back kick one leg over the opposite shoulder. Roll back, keeping your hips off the floor by using the other leg to push your hips up. Switch legs and repeat on other side.

Timing –

1, 2, and.

Back Rock Low

Action –

Lower version of the Back Rock. Same action but breaker is playing with the levels in the move.

Timing –

1, and 2.

Freezes Still positions

Air Baby (High Chair)

Action – One hand is placed on the floor in front of the same leg, and that leg is placed on the elbow of the placed hand arm. The arm needs to be vertical from wrist to elbow. The head is straight at a 45 degree angle off the floor, with the other arm place in line with the head to prevent crashing your head to the floor.

Variation - Reverse Air Baby

Action – One hand is placed on the floor. Put the same foot as your arm on the forearm, then push your hips in the air with your free arm pulling away to create counterbalance.

Air Chair

Your elbow is placed into the lower back / top of the hip with your head off the floor. Both legs are up in a straight line making a V shape up to the sky.

Variation - Side Air Chair

Your elbow is placed into the lower back / top of the hip with your head off the floor and both legs in a straight line, horizontal with your head.

Air Freeze (one-handed handstand)

With one arm on the floor, hold the other arm out to the side to create counterbalance. Kick both legs in the air in a straight line.

Variation - Air Freeze with hooked legs

With one arm on the floor, hold the other arm out to the side to create a counterbalance. Kick both legs in the air into a hooked shape to hold.

Baby Freeze (Handglide Freeze)

Action – Use the elbow of one arm and place in next to the belly button. Place the hand of this arm on the floor. The opposite arm is on a diagonal line in alignment with the other hand. Raise both feet off the ground and the weight remains in the stabbing elbow not on the head or face.

Baby Variation (scissor kicks)

Action – Use the elbow of one arm and place in next to the belly button. Place the hand of this arm on the floor. The opposite arm is on a diagonal line in alignment with the other hand. Raise both feet off the ground, one foot more forward than the other, with one knee in contact with the non-stabbing arm (either leg can be in contact with the non-stabbing arm), and the weight remains in the stabbing elbow not on the head or face. Switch legs.

Closed Baby

Action – From Stab, underneath leg makes contact with non-stabbing arm.

Open Baby

Action – From Stab, top leg makes contact with non-stabbing arm.

Back Baby

Action – Similar to Shoulder Freeze, roll back onto one shoulder, keeping both knees bent and one knee in contact with one elbow. Switch legs.

Baby Variations

Experimenting with different leg shapes creates new baby freezes.

Back Chair

Action – Place the palm of one hand on the lower back / top of the same hip. Shoulders on the floor, elbow of the hand on the floor, raise your legs above the hand and hip.

Variation – one foot on the floor.

Bridge

Action – Both feet on the floor, both hands raised over the head, palms touching the floor either side of the head. Push your hips to ceiling, arching back, and ensure feet push into shoulders to gain shoulder flexibility.

Variation – Take one foot off the floor, extend to ceiling or cross over the other knee.

Variation – Head Bridge, both feet on the floor, arms crossed across body, push hips to the ceiling, weight on both feet and top of the head. Ensure weight remains more into the feet to reduce pressure on the neck.

Chair Freeze

Action – Your elbow is placed into the lower back / top of the hip. Your hand is placed on the floor and the elbow connected to the back is vertical to the ceiling. Rotate your hips so both are facing up to the ceiling. Keep the opposite foot in contact with the floor, lift the same leg as your arm is balanced on, cross the foot over the supporting knee.

Variation – Both feet stay on the floor.

Variation – Air Chair. Both feet and head come off the floor.

History - credited to Ronnie Rob of the Baby Zulu Kings.

Dead Roach

Action – Both forearms connect and elbows come into the abdominals. Both palms are on the floor, both knees bend in and turn out away from each other to make the body as small and possible. Lift both knees off the floor, with your forehead staying in contact with the ground.

Figure 4 Freeze (Buck 4)

Action – Lying on your back, arms out to the sides. One foot is in contact with the floor, and push your knee and both hips to the sky. The other leg crosses the ankle over the raised knee of the supporting leg making a '4' shape with the legs.

Forearm Freeze

Action – With one forearm on the floor at a 45-degree angle, and the other hand in a diagonal position from the forearm, kick both legs up into the air and try to balance.

Variation - One-armed Forearm Freeze

Action – With one forearm on the floor at a 45-degree angle, kick both legs up into the air and try to balance.

Halo

Action – From Stab twist as though you are going to Chair Freeze but lift both legs up into a high V sending them out wide to counterbalance. Use the non-stabbing arm to balance, placing it behind the head.

Head Hollowback

Action – Make a triangle with your hands and your head. Make sure you are on the top of your head then try and lift your knees one knee closer to the floor, the other lifted towards the face.

Headstand

Action – Make a triangle with your hands and your head. Make sure you are on the top of your head then try and lift your knees into a V position.

Head Invert

Action – Make a triangle with your hands and your head. Make sure you are on the top of your head then try and lift your legs off the floor.

High Leg Locks

Action – In a handstand, wrap one leg around the other knee, keeping both legs bent to lock them into each other.

Hollowbacks

Action – From a straight handstand push your head and chest in a straight line forwards and push your hips up to the ceiling as you lengthen your legs away from you to create a counterbalance.

Variation – Single-leg Hollowbacks

Action – From a straight handstand push your head and chest in a straight line forwards and push your hips up to the ceiling. One leg is towards the ceiling the other dropping to the floor behind your head to create a counterbalance.

Hong 10

Action – From Chair Stab position, the non-stabbing arm goes behind your head to help you balance. Legs stretch away, each low to the ground but off the floor.

Inverts

Action – From handstand push gluteus maximus over hands and beyond, lower feet towards your face to counterbalance.

Knee Pose

Action - One knee is on the floor, and one foot is on the floor. The knee is bent at a 90-degree angle, with your forearms resting on the thighs, and your hands in different positions.

Pencil Freeze

Action – Make a triangle with your hands and your head. Make sure you are on the top of your head then take your legs up into a straight line towards the ceiling. Your arms come into the side of your body pushing in and up to the ceiling.

Shoulder Freeze

Action – Lying on one shoulder. Place one hand in front of the face to stabilise balance. Push both hips up to the ceiling making contact with the stabilising arm.

Side Chair (Flat)

Action – Your elbow is placed at the side of the hip, and the palm of that hand is placed on the floor. The forearm is vertical, and the head and feet extend away from each other and all come off the floor. Your legs stay bent and your other arm reaches up to gain balance.

Scissor Freeze

Action – From Stab, the same leg as your stabbing arm is in front. Your top leg is twisting back and bent reaching towards the floor but not touching it.

Spiders

Action – Both arms swing under the knees, palms are in contact with the floor. Your knees balance on both elbows, and your feet come off the floor.

Turtle Freeze

Action – Similar to the Dead Roach, but only your hands stay in contact with the floor. Both hands are in contact with the ground, your forearms are vertical and your elbows are in contact with your hips to lift both feet and your head off the floor.

W-Freeze

Action – The balls of your feet stay in contact with the floor. Both your knees drop forward, hips are pushed forwards, and one hand stays in contact with the ground behind the hips.
Variation – Both hands stay in contact with the ground.

Tricks

Actions are generally inspired by gymnastics, free-running or martial arts. Tricks are generally taught with a spotter, mats, and we highly recommend working on these actions with a UK Breakin' teacher, because these moves come with higher risks. The popular tricks include those listed below.

Trac 2 is credited for putting gymnastics into Breakin' "I incorporated gymnastics into the dance...I didn't put dance into gymnastics" *(Schloss 2009, Foundations)*.

Aerial
No-handed cartwheel.

B Twist / Butterfly Twist
A butterfly kick, with a 360-degree horizontal twist.

Back Flick / Back Handspring

A backwards rotation with hands making contact with the ground during the rotation.

Baby – Pommel Twist
– Kip Up (watch your fingers)

From stab position swing both legs around, from the back circling away from stabbing arm. As legs reach the front, both arms are on the floor behind providing base (stay in a tucked shape). On completing circle catch in stab to finish pommel, then collapse on to your back into kip up.
Timing –
1, 2, 3, 4, 5, 6.

Back Tuck / Back Flip

A backward rotation, where the hands do not make contact with the floor, legs are together and tucked.

Bronco – Standing

Action –

From standing position, bend both knees, jump into Canal Ball position (like a wheelbarrow position without someone holding your feet) and then back into the squat position.

Timing –

and 1, 2.

Variations –

Can land on one hand or forearms. Can add clap when travelling between feet and landing on hands.

Circular Front Rolls
Action –
Often done using four forward rolls. The circular forward rolls link together to the four corners to complete the circle. The forward rolls require the breaker to touch their chin to their chest as they roll and to land on the upper blades of their shoulder blades – not the flat of their back – to make the move roll through the spine.

Timing –
1, 2, 3, 4.

Flash Kicks
A backward rotation, where the hands do not make contact with the floor, legs are apart.

Headspring
A forward rotation, using gentle contact with the hands and head mid-way through rotation.

Variation –
No-Handed Headspring.

Loser

A forward rotation made while the body travels backwards.

Raiz

A side twist with legs creating an arch shape.

Side Flips

A sideways rotation keeping legs tucked.

Webster

A forwards rotation guided by a swinging leg.

Powermoves

Dynamic movements which generally rotate / leave the floor.

Power moves come with a greater risk of injury, so we advise you to learn these with a Breakin' teacher at a UK Breakin' hub. There are certain conditioning exercises for each move.

Airflare

Actions –

Starting feet apart, take a hand across the body placing it on the floor to replace the opposite foot. That foot extends back on a 45-degree angle extending into the air. The other leg leaves the floor and extends straight up to begin to circle. The other hand makes contact with the ground. The first arm which made contact rotates 360-degrees around the body to place back on the floor allowing the legs to stay in the air, to continue the rotation.

Risks –

Your wrists, elbows and shoulders are most at risk.
When learning, breakers can land heavily on ankles and knees, putting pressure on hips. Joint-strengthening exercises are advised before training Airflares.
Ribs and torso needs to rotate quickly, so training the rotation in handstand before training at speed is advised.

History –

Pioneers: Pablo Flores 1998, also known as Air Tracks and Swipes.

Back Spin

Actions –

Cali Whip version. Start in James Brown splits, one leg extended forwards the other bent back, same arm as extended leg on the ground. Kick the bent leg across the body and arm circles with the leg across and above the body. Apply pressure using the hand in contact with the ground and lying onto the back, raise your head off the floor and bring your knees and arms together to make the smallest possible contact with the ground on your back (Dead Bug / Tuck position) (mid-position of the back).

Risks –

To avoid unnecessary tension on the head, contract from the abdominals to lift your head by using your core muscles to control the lifting of your head .

Variations –

You can get into the move from sitting, from Stab, from standing. Add hops to the backspin.

History -

Most likely one of the first Power moves.

Baby Swipe

Actions –

Starting with both feet on the floor, and both hands behind the hips on the ground. Take one hand across the body and twist the hips at the same time to twist towards the floor, taking both feet off the ground and landing back in the starting position. The feet travel in a box landing corner to corner, so each finishing position will face a different direction.

Variations –

One leg stays on the floor.

Baby Starlights – Same action, but don't change direction as you land.

Belly Spin

Actions –

Lie on your stomach, lift your arms and legs off the floor and spin either anti-clockwise or clockwise. You commonly use your arms to gain momentum before lifting both off the ground.

Risks –

Head colliding with the ground, bruised ribs. Consider the best Go Downs to prevent injury.

Variations –

One leg stays on the floor.

Baby Starlights – Same action, but don't change direction as you land.

Bullets

Actions –

From Stab, kick your leg around as if going into a windmill. Make more of a rotation to be able to push off your shoulders. Bring legs together and arms by your side to make a tight, straight line to make a 360-degree rotation to land on your back.

Risks –

Head colliding with the ground.

Bum Spin

Actions –

Sit on your gluteus maximus, take your feet off the floor, and keep your knees bent. Use your arms to start the turning momentum and lift them off the ground.

Crazy Turtles

Actions –

Start in Stab, tap the other arm forward, swap onto the other arm to stab and tap the free arm, swap to repeat.

Crickets

Actions –

From Stab position, turn by using the other hand in front of the head to pull and create the rotation, and to allow the stab arm to hop, while the hips and legs kick to help create the hop.

Circles (Ground Flairs)

Actions –

Both legs circle together 360-degrees, starting from the back and returning legs to the back.

Variation –

Start action from the Stab position. Turning variation pommel twists.

Criticals

Actions –

Starts from Stab. Your legs start to circle in the air, and when the legs reach the front the non-stabbing arm circles around the body to land back in Stab.

Risks –

The wrists, elbows and shoulders are most at risk, so conditioning and strengthening exercises are needed to prepare for training Criticals.

Falling and landing uncomfortably on your hips, shoulders and potentially head is possible. It is advised to train on mats to soften your landing.

Dark Hammers

Actions –

Start in Stab on one arm, swap onto the other arm and repeat.

Elbow Spin

Actions –

From Elbow Freeze, use your free arm to create momentum and rotate using taps to spin freely.

Risks –

Collapsing into the neck. You need to think about pushing your shoulders away from the floor as you spin.

Elbow Tracks

Actions –

One hand is placed on the floor and on the opposite arm the whole forearm is in contact with the floor. Swing legs from low to high, one leg following the other. When your legs are at the highest point, your body twists anti-clockwise to land on the opposite elbow.

Risks –

There's a potential risk to land on your head or neck. You are aiming to feel you are pushing your shoulders away from the floor.

Variations –

Start in Elbow Stand.

Flares

Actions –

One hand is placed on the floor slightly in front of the body. One leg travels behind the other, and both arms move to behind the back and both legs circle in front of the body in a high V. The circle continues, hands are in handstand position and legs continue the circle.

Variations –

- **New York Entry Flare – actions start from a kick.**
- **Chair Flares – start from Chair Freeze, legs circle back and land in Chair Freeze on the opposite side.**
- **Forearm Flares – as the arms reach back instead of landing on hands, land on forearms and circle legs around.**

History –

Inspired by a gymnast called Kurt Thomas from the USA.

Halo (No-Handed Tracks)

Actions –

From Stab, place your head on the floor. Kick the same leg and stabbing arm in front of the body, lift the other arm up and back, so the other arm follows and land back in the Stab. Keep legs off the floor. The spin must be at 45 degrees to be a Halo.

Risks –

Neck strain and dislocated vertebra. Neck conditioning with UK Breakin' hubs is advised. Having a strong Chair Freeze is compulsory before training this move.

Handglide
(legs and arms wide and open
– slowly drag and crunch in)

Actions –

From Stab position, reach the non-stabbing arm above the head, bent and the hand ready to pull away from the body to start the rotation. Keep legs bent in frog position.

Risks –

Wrists take a lot of the pressure in this move. You need to use the correct flooring to make sure the floor doesn't over grip and prevent the rotation.

Variations –

Spin in different Freezes: Chair Freeze, Side Chair, Lotus Position, Icey Ice, Air Baby, Superman, etc.

History –

Using an umbrella!

Head Spin

Actions –

Start in a Headstand. Your legs initially are bent, and use your hands in contact with the ground to rotate the body. Use two hands from one side of the face and drag the head to face the hands, repeat to spin without the hands.

Risks –

Balding! To reduce damage to your hair using a headspin cap or hat, and treat the scalp to prevent calluses.

Variations –

Advanced – the upper body begins to spin and legs follow kicking to offer more spin

History –

Swan from Mighty Zulu Kings is credited for doing the first one shot headspins in Breakin'.
The first person to do a continuous head spin was Kid Freeze. Float and Orko contributed to the development of the techniques.
Tony the Pencil from Second to None came up with the idea for continuous drills by watching the ice skaters. Then in 1988 did his first one over 10 turns out of a normal glide. He realised he could carry on by using his arms to steer himself while practicing in the YMCA in Bournemouth.

Head Swipe (neck move - Twists)

Actions –

Start in Turtle Freeze. Rotate into a Head Bridge, keep both feet off the floor, and rotate back into a Turtle Freeze. Turning either clockwise or anti-clockwise.

Risks –

Not turning your head will lead to neck strain. Also wrist strain from overuse or miss-catching.

Variations –

Half-Head Swipe from back to Baby Freeze. Chair Freeze to Chair Freeze. Take one foot off the floor.

Jack Hammer

Actions –

From Stab position but with your free arm tucked behind your back. Use the momentum from hips / legs to hop on stabbing arm and rotate.

Risks –

Using the Stab position can be uncomfortable. More research is needed to find ways to prevent injury.

Munch Mills (Baby Mills)

Actions –

Similar to Windmills but with leg crosses. Starting on your back, arms rotated and hands in fists, legs crossed at the ankles and knees.

History –

Created by Oz Rock.

Power Prep / New Yorkers / 50p

Actions –

Your opposite hand goes onto the floor next to your opposite foot. Kick that foot into the air, place the other hand onto the floor and kick the other leg into the air. Repeat and rotate, with your leg travelling around your hands.

Swipes

Actions –

From Power Prep, the same arm as your leg takes the body weight, as the opposite arm reaches to the side rotating the body. Your leg continues rotating and staying in the air as you switch arms again ready to repeat. The supporting leg rotates with each landing traveling to four corners.

Turtles

Actions –

In Turtle Freeze extend one arm and transfer your body weight onto it, bringing the other along with the body. Your whole body will rotate as you repeat.

Windmills

Actions –

From James Brown position, both legs circle one after the other. Lift into Stab position, and continue the circling of the legs. Collapse from the stabbing arm and continue rotation.

Risks –

Shoulder burns and bruising. Wearing spin tops to allow for guiding is important.

Variations –

Australia Mills
Barrell Mills (no-handed)
Grab Mills
Handcuff Mills
Magnet Mills
Nut Crackers
Planch Mills
Shoulder Fly Mills
Superman Mills (Stretch Mills)
Tap Mills
Tombstones
(Descriptions can be found on the following pages)

Windmill variations -

Australia Mills

Action – A traditional Windmill while holding your legs in the figure '4' position.

Barrel Mills (no-handed)

Action – A traditional Windmill but arms and legs wider as though the breaker is holding a barrel.

Grab Mills

Action – A traditional Windmill with breaker holding onto the leg of the stabbing arm.

Handcuff Mills

Action – A traditional Windmill with arms behind the back as if in handcuffs.

Windmill variations

Magnet Mills

Action – Similar to Barrel Mills but with arms even more rounded to increase speed and fluidity, the rotation should be around the head, not shoulders.

Nutcrackers

Action – A traditional Windmill with breaker holding onto the groin.

Planch Mill

Action – As you rotate push up into both hands and try to make a straight line with both arms and legs.

Superman Mills (Stretch Mills)

Action – As you rotate to the front, push both hands onto the floor above head, send legs wide and then rotate onto back to repeat.

Windmill variations

Tap Mills (webs)

Action – A traditional Windmill, where one foot makes contact with the ground to assist the rotation each time.
We have seen a high injury rate with this move and would advise against it.

Tombstones

Action – A traditional Windmill with legs together, piked above head as you rotate.

UFO Handglides

Actions –

From standing, place one hand on the floor as you lower your body. Your other arm makes contact with the ground. Keep your arms straight, head leaning forwards so hips can be above hands and both feet off the floor and slightly spread. Continue to transfer weight between each hand to rotate in a circle.

History -

Bboy Freeze fine from Second to None created a variation of UFO's done to the side called Future Floors.

90's

Actions –

A one-handed handstand rotating clockwise.

Variation -

Using the same arm as before but spinning anti-clockwise.

2000's

Actions –

Place one hand on top of the other while moving into a handstand and spin upside down, either clockwise or anticlockwise.

Cool Down Exercises
Actions to prevent injury and prepare the body for post-training rest.

These are generic ideas for cooling down. More research into the best exercises is needed, to give scientific evidence for the best recovery exercises.

Actions –

Stretching neck, shoulders, elbows and wrists with both dynamic and static stretches. Remember to do the stretches on both sides to balance the body.

Actions –

Mobilising and relaxing the back in cobra and child's pose, moving between the positions, and relaxing your breathing to bring your heart rate back to your resting heart rate.

Actions –

Mobilising and stretching hips, lumbar spine, hamstrings, quadriceps, knees, gastrocnemius (calves), ankles, and feet. Use a mix of static and dynamic stretches and gentle mobilising exercises.

After exercises make sure you drink to remain hydrated, and layer up with clothing to allow muscles to cool down slowly. Take showers / baths to aid recovery. Get plenty of sleep for whole-body recovery.

Training Journals
Recording training to find out how you achieve the best outcome

Time –

Scheduling the best time to train. Recording the day of the week, the time of day, and how you felt, to discover the best time for you to train.

Diet –

Record what you eat the day before, the day of training and how much energy you had in the session to be able to understand the food and water needs of your body to build productive training sessions.

Clothing –

What are you using for the moves you are performing e.g. spin hats, spin tops? What are you wearing to suit the temperature of the place where you are training?

Type of training –

Mind training – listening to music that inspires you to be creative, that inspires you to drill and condition. Physical sessions – including drill sessions working on technique, creative sessions developing characters and stories, conditioning sessions working on stamina, explosive power, and flexibility.

Move progressions –

Recording what moves you want to work on and how you are developing with that move.

Combinations –

What combinations did you create in that session? How did they flow? How did they look, and how did they feel? What reaction did you get from your crew?

Image and video footage –

Recording sessions and rounds on video to analyse what is going right and where you need to make improvements. Break down the creativity from standing on the side of the battle until you leave to analyse different actions.

Space for reflection

Space for reflection

Space for reflection

Space for reflection

References

BOOKS

Chang J, 2007, Can't Stop won't Stop, Edition 2, Ebury Press, UK
Joseph G Schloss, 2009, Foundations, Oxford University Press, New York

WEBSITES

https://thebreaks.org/ 10/08/2021
https://www.societydanceacademy.com/the-pioneers 10/08/2021

PEOPLE

We want to give a shout out to UK Breakin' members who worked to develop this first edition, including: Omar "Kidd Ronin" Spence Reckless Wolverhampton, James "Veeza" Williams Gloucestershire, James "the Robot/Foggy" Forgerty Leeds, Sunanda "Sunsun" Biswas London, Tim "Lil'Tim" Hamilton London/Bournemouth, Tom "Tozz" Glynn St Helens, Tony "the Pencil" Penfold Bournemouth, Michael "Silence" Glasgow Birmingham, Rachel "Welsh Poppy" Pedley Rhondda, Jamie "Flexton" Berry Swindon/Wales, who have shared their knowledge, skills, reached out to the community to hear more voices and developed the book to share their knowledge with others and future breakers.
Including all the breakers included in the photos:
BGirl Labrynth
BGirl Solid
BBoy AJ Cypher Cat
BBoy Jem
BBoy Litefoot
BBoy Lotus
BBoy Tytan
and to the classes who tested the content before going to print Motion Control Dance, Breakinburgh and UC Crew.

References - Danceacise

BBoy Lil'Tim is a UK Breakin' legend, the first UK BBoy to represent the UK at the international competition RedBull BC One.

BBoy Lil'Tim has been teaching and judging for over 30 years. Noticing a need for a training mat to improve the positions of Breakin' moves, he started making plans to develop the mat in 1997. By 2007 the first mat was designed with New York train and subway signs embedded in the design.

 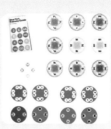  

Lil'Tim and Denis Armit designed and developed the Danceacise and Breakacise mat in 2014 which is the mat in use now.

We have used the Danceacise and Breakacise mat to help demonstrate the positions needed to perform the moves safely.

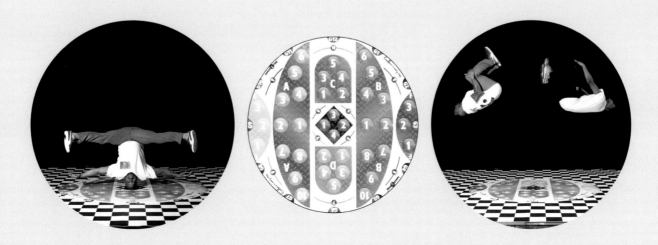

Arts Council England

<u>Funding</u>

Arts Council England supported this Glossary of Terms by providing finances to UK Breakin' for the consultations, photography, supporting videos and music.

We know that Breakin' is a profession, so all who were given contracts were paid wages based on One Dance UK's rates.

As part of this process, we have been discussing fair pay, social justice, equality, diversity, inclusion, climate impact and we are looking to improve culture sector employment.

To join us in these discussions email: info@ukbreakin.org